YORKSHIRE
RECIPES

AN OUTSTANDING COLLECTION OF
YORKSHIRE'S FINEST RECIPES

JOSEPHINE BLYTH

AN INTRODUCTION

Yorkshire is God's own county. The land is sweet and good. The people are canny and creative; they make great use of the food they produce. To discover the best Yorkshire recipes, I'd recommend that you explore the place, with its rural and urban landscapes as well as its seascapes. Visit the hostelries, farms, tradespeople and artisans. Sample the breadth of delicacies. You'll be inspired to make your own authentic feasts, as I have been.

Plan picnics packed with Yorkshire fruit, vegetables, meat, fish and cheese. Give your inner baker free rein to make traditional puddings, bread, cakes and buns. Your friends and family will be delighted with your endeavours.

Josephine
Blyth

SAVOURY RECIPES

BRIGHOUSE SPRINKLES

serves about 8, for a little snack

These add a crunch to a salad, or you could nibble on them with a glass of something. In my family they are known as 'taste sensations'.

- 100g sunflower seeds
- 2 tablespoons Tamari or Shoyu (Japanese soy sauce)

Toast the sunflower seeds in a dry frying pan over a very low heat; pay close attention all the time, as they burn easily, turning them regularly. As soon as you detect a toasty smell, pour in the Tamari and stir until all the seeds are coated. Keep on pushing them around the pan with a wooden spatula until the sauce has evaporated. This prevents them from sticking and takes a little effort.

Spoon them into a bowl and eat as soon as they are cool enough, or store in a sealed jar for a few days.

BUTTERSHAW GARLIC & CORIANDER NAAN BREAD

makes 4 large or 8 mini naans

- 310g strong, white bread flour
- 1 teaspoon dried fast action yeast
- 1 teaspoon sea salt
- ½ teaspoon sugar
- ¼ teaspoon nigella seeds
- 2 tablespoons fresh coriander, *finely chopped*
- 2 tablespoons sunflower oil and a little extra for kneading
- 2 teaspoons plain yoghurt
- 140ml warm water

For the garlic and coriander butter:
- 50g salted butter
- 4 cloves garlic, *finely sliced*

Preheat the oven to 230°C/450°F. In a large bowl, combine the flour, yeast, sea salt, sugar, nigella seeds and 1 tablespoon finely chopped coriander. Make a well in the centre and add the oil, yoghurt and water.

Using your hands, bring the dough together. Knead for 5 minutes. If the dough feels sticky, oil your hands and continue kneading.

Grease the bowl and cover with a damp tea towel before leaving to rise in a warm place for 1 hour.

Meanwhile, melt the butter in a small pan, add the finely sliced garlic and fry until aromatic. Add the remaining chopped coriander and set aside until needed.

Knock the air out of the naan dough and divide into four equal portions (or eight if you prefer mini naans). Take one piece of dough, roll into a ball and, using a rolling pin, roll your naan until it's around 1cm in thickness. Take one end and pull into a teardrop shape.

Cook the dough, either by grilling for 1 minute on both sides or bake in a preheated oven at 230°C/450°F until golden brown. Once cooked, brush with the garlic butter and serve immediately. *Note: these may be kept warm by wrapping them in foil.*

PIES

The first purpose of pie was to carry food out to the fields. Pastry was a cheaper, more nutritious and delicious packaging than a dish. As industry and mining grew, pies fed these workers too. The truth that Yorkshire people embody stolid practicality and simple delight is exemplified in pies.

It is said that pies have a hallowed place on the Yorkshire table, so if you want to eat really good pies – the world's best pies – you know where to go.

CHERRY BURTON CHICKEN, BACON, LEEK & MUSHROOM PIE

serves 4

- 4 skinless chicken breasts, or 8 skinless, boneless thighs
- juice of half a lemon
- 2 tablespoons olive or sunflower oil
- freshly ground sea salt and black pepper
- 4 rashers of bacon, *rolled up and each cut into 3*
- 1 large onion
- 4 cloves garlic, *crushed and finely chopped*
- 2 sticks celery, *finely chopped*
- 2 leeks, *shredded*
- 14 to 16 button mushrooms, *chopped*
- 450ml stock - ham and chicken
- 1 teaspoon Marigold Bouillon powder
- leaves from 5 or 6 stalks of thyme
- 1 handful of chopped parsley
- 300ml tub crème fraîche

Preheat the oven to 200°C/400°F.

You will need a deep pie dish or four individual plate sized *Yorkshire Puddings* (page 27).

Cut the chicken into bite-sized pieces. Season it with salt and pepper and leave to marinate in the lemon and oil while you chop up the vegetables and herbs. In a heavy-based saucepan, brown the chicken and bacon rolls, for 3 minutes on each side. Put the chicken on a clean dish and set aside leaving the bacon in the pan. Fry the onions with the bacon until they are transparent or just starting to brown; add the garlic, fry until fragrant and add the celery, leeks and mushrooms. Cook, stirring frequently, until softened.

Stir in the chicken with the stock and simmer on the hob for 20 minutes or until the chicken is cooked through, before seasoning the sauce with the Bouillon powder, pepper and a little salt, if needed. Add the crème fraîche and stir well.

Fill a deep pie dish to serve four and top with an *Aberford Pie Crust* (page 30) before cooking at 200°C/400°F for 20 minutes or until golden brown.

Alternatively, fill four individual plate sized *Yorkshire Puddings* (page 27) and serve immediately.

CHICKEN TIKKA MASALA FROM MICKELTHWAITE

serves 4

Bradford has been voted curry capital of the world so curry must be as Yorkshire as it is Indian! When the woollen mills were booming, the former British colonies provided cheap labour. As well as cloth, these new Yorkshire residents wove exotic spices into the city's diet.

For the chicken marinade:
- 800g boneless and skinless chicken thighs, *cut into bite-sized pieces*
- 1 cup plain yogurt
- 1½ tablespoons minced garlic
- 1 tablespoon minced fresh root ginger
- 2 teaspoons garam masala
- 1 teaspoon turmeric
- 1 teaspoon ground cumin
- ¼ teaspoon ground red chili powder
- 1 teaspoon of salt

For the sauce:
- 2 tablespoons of vegetable oil
- 2 tablespoons butter
- 2 small onions (or 1 large onion), *finely diced*

- 3 cloves garlic, *crushed and finely chopped*
- 1 tablespoon ginger, *finely grated*
- 1½ teaspoons garam masala
- 1½ teaspoons ground cumin
- 1 teaspoon turmeric powder
- 1 teaspoon ground coriander
- 400g liquidised tinned tomatoes in juice
- 80ml to 100ml chicken stock
- 1 teaspoon chilli powder
- 1 teaspoon salt
- 1 x 300ml pot crème fraîche
- 1 teaspoon brown sugar
- ¼ cup water if needed
- 4 tablespoons fresh coriander, *to garnish*

In a large bowl, combine the chicken with all of the ingredients for the chicken marinade; let it marinate for at least 10 minutes, or ideally overnight.

When you're ready to cook, heat the oil in a large heavy based pan until sizzling, then add the chicken pieces in batches of two or three, making sure not to crowd the pan. Fry until browned around 3 minutes on each side. Set aside and keep warm. You will finish cooking the chicken in the sauce.

Melt the butter in the same pan. Fry the onions until soft (about 3 minutes) while scraping up any browned bits stuck on the bottom of the pan. Add the garlic and ginger and sauté for 1 minute until fragrant, then add the garam masala, cumin, turmeric and coriander. Fry for a further 20 seconds until the spices begin to release their amazing scent, while stirring occasionally.

Add the tomato puree, 80ml chicken stock, chilli powder and salt. Stir well and simmer for 10 to 15 minutes until the sauce thickens and becomes a deep brown red colour. Stir occasionally to make sure nothing sticks to the pan.

Stir the cream and sugar through the sauce. Add the chicken and its juices back into the pan and cook for an additional 10 minutes or until the chicken is cooked through and the sauce is thick and bubbling. Pour in more stock or water to thin out the sauce, if needed.

Garnish with coriander and serve with fresh, hot basmati rice, or *Chickpea Pilau Rice* (see below).

CHICKPEA PILAU RICE FROM PEEL PARK

serves 6 to 8

- 450g basmati rice
- 4 to 5 tablespoons oil
- 25g butter
- I small onion, *finely sliced*
- 2 to 3 teaspoons salt
- I green chilli
- 6 cloves
- I teaspoon coriander seeds
- I to 2 teaspoons cumin seeds
- ½ teaspoon black peppercorns
- 3 cardamom pods
- I cinnamon sticks
- water (double the volume of the rice)
- 500g tinned chickpeas, *rinsed*

Gently wash the rice in cold water until the water runs clear; this removes the starch and makes sure the rice isn't sticky once cooked. Leave it to soak in cold water.

Put the oil, butter and onion in a pan and fry over a medium heat until the onion is see-through. Add all the spices and stir for a minute, followed by a couple tablespoonfuls of water. Add the chickpeas and stir again. Add the remaining water and bring to the boil. Taste the stock, adjust the seasoning if necessary, before carefully stirring in the rice.

Bring the rice to the boil, then turn the heat right down and put the lid on. Allow the rice to cook for approximately 15 to 20 minutes. Stir cautiously once. You will know the rice is cooked when you roll a few grains between your thumb and forefinger – if there's any hardness, replace the lid and cook a little longer until it's soft. Serve with curry and *Particularly Delicious Apple Chutney* (page 15) or cucumber and mint yoghurt.

FILEY
FISH PIE
serves 6

I love a highly textured fish pie. I'd go so far as to say it is my favourite meal. In my opinion, it must contain eggs & smoked fish, but not prawns or other shellfish. Jamie Oliver taught me to include vegetables in the pie and Anton Mosimann not to overcook the fish. I love chatting to the staff on the fish counter about what they'd recommend; a variety of colours and textures is best, e.g. Salmon, Pollock, Ling, Gurnard – the list is endless. You don't need to choose the most frequently used, predictable fish. Ask your fish monger to fillet them too; choking on fish bones is highly undesirable!

- 600g assorted fish with at least 200g being smoked
- juice of 1 lemon
- 100g potatoes (1kg before peeling)
- 2 large free-range eggs
- 300g spinach
- 30g butter
- a glug of milk
- 2 tablespoons light olive oil

- 1 large onion, *finely chopped*
- 2 cloves garlic, *crushed and minced*
- 2 medium carrots, *peeled and cut into slim sticks, 4cm long*
- 300ml crème fraîche
- 200g grated cheddar cheese
- 1 heaped teaspoon wholegrain mustard
- juice of half a lemon
- 1 large handful chopped parsley

You will need a deep pie dish. Preheat the oven to 190°C/375°F.

Place the fish in a large dish and squeeze the juice of a lemon over it; generously season with freshly ground black pepper and some sea salt. Leave it to marinade while you prepare the rest of the pie.

Peel the potatoes, cut them into small pieces and place in a large pan of cold salted water. Bring to the boil and cook for 2 minutes. Add the eggs and boil for 6 more minutes. Wash the spinach thoroughly, before lightly steaming it for a further 2 to 3 minutes or until it begins to wilt. Remove the eggs, plunge them into cold water and leave to cool completely. Drain the potatoes and mash them with generous quantities of butter, sea salt and black pepper (and milk if needed). Press the spinach through a sieve to remove as much excess liquid as you can before adding butter and seasoning.

Warm 2 tablespoons of extra virgin oil in a frying pan, cook the onion gently, add the garlic and sliced carrots and cook, covered, for around 5 minutes. Remove from the heat and add the crème fraîche, 2 handfuls of grated cheese (reserving about a third of it separately, to melt on top of the pie, if you wish), mustard, lemon juice and parsley. Stir thoroughly. In a large, deep pie dish, make a base layer of spinach; add the marinated fish on top. Peel and quarter the eggs and arrange evenly amidst the fish. Pour/spoon the saucy mixture over everything. Top with the mashed potato and a bit of extra grated cheese, if you wish.

Bake at 190°C/375°F for 25 to 30 minutes or until bubbling beautifully around the edges.

Serve with an assortment of green vegetables: peas and green beans are a must. A glass or two of dry white wine will help matters too. Ideal eaten with a view of the sea.

HARROGATE BLUE CHEESE & WALNUT QUICHE

serves 6

For the pastry:
- 175g plain flour
- 1 pinch of salt
- 85g butter, *cut into tiny cubes & chilled*
- a little cold water to mix

For the filling:
- 1 onion, *chopped*
- 2 tablespoons light olive oil
- 2 sticks celery
- 2 medium free-range eggs, *lightly beaten*

- 1 x 300ml pot crème fraîche
- 110g Harrogate Blue cheese, *grated*
- 110g walnuts, *finely chopped*
- 1 large handful parsley, *finely chopped*

You will need two 22cm loose-based tins. Preheat the oven to 180°C/350°F.

Sieve the flour and salt into a large mixing bowl, before rubbing the butter in until it resembles breadcrumbs. Add enough water to bring the mixture together into a dough that is soft but not sticky. Chill it in the fridge to rest before rolling.

Roll out the pastry and use to line two 22cm loose bottomed flan tins. Bake the pastry cases blind at 180°C/350°F for 15 minutes on the middle shelf of the oven.

Lightly beat the eggs. Take the pastry case out of the oven and paint the inside with the beaten egg. Bake for a further 5 minutes before leaving to cool.

Fry the onion in olive oil until transparent. Add the celery and sweat until softened before allowing to cool a little. Combine the eggs and crème fraîche, mix in the onions, celery, blue cheese, walnuts and parsley. Pour the filling into the pastry cases and bake at 180°C/350°F for 30 to 40 minutes, or until your quiche is golden brown and puffy.

© Silvia Ramos

HAVERBREAD (SOFT OATCAKES)

makes 8 to 10 wraps

This is a Yorkshire speciality from the days when oats, not wheat, were the staple grain. This is not a recipe for the crunchy oatcakes we know from Scotland. It's a soft pancakey bread. Haver is an old-fashioned name for oats, therefore a haversack was what you used to carry the oats home from the mill. My dad always called packed lunches 'haversack rations'. Pop a wrap, or two, filled with Yorkshire cheese, ham and salad in your lunchbox, & carry it on a day out.

- 1 sachet 7g dried yeast
- 225g fine oatmeal
- 225g plain white flour
- 1 teaspoon salt
- 1 teaspoon sugar
- 850ml warm milk and water
- a little oil or butter for lightly frying

In a large mixing bowl, combine all the dry ingredients; be careful not to let the salt touch the yeast as this can kill the yeast. Pour in the warm liquid and whizz it up with an electric hand whisk. Cover this batter with a clean tea towel and leave at warm room temperature until it is thick. Beat smooth again.

Heat a heavy based frying pan or griddle to a high heat. Lightly grease the surface. Ladle out a scoop of mixture, pour it into the pan in either small cakes (for *Whitby Smoked Mackerel Pâté*, page 24) or spread it out with the base of the ladle into a big circle for wraps. Cook for 2 to 3 minutes, then turn it over. Cook the second side for 1 to 2 minutes. These makes excellent biscuits and wraps for cheeses and salad.

Traditionally these were hung out to dry on the laundry airer hanging from the kitchen ceiling, so if you didn't eat the whole batch fresh, you toasted the dried ones.

LAWN MOWINGS' PIE

serves 6

This is a spinach quiche. It was given its name by a very rude party guest who had arrived late for a buffet. Peering down the table disparagingly she told her husband "nothing much left, just a bit of Lawn Mowing Pie." I think this is the perfect dish for a picnic, in sight of a village cricket match, in honour of the groundsmen who keep Yorkshire cricket pitches in fabulous nick.

For the shortcrust pastry:
- 240g wholemeal plain flour
- 120g butter
- cold water to mix

For the filling:
- 450g bag spinach
- ¼ teaspoon nutmeg, *freshly grated*
- 1 large onion, *finely chopped*

- olive oil
- 2 to 3 cloves garlic, *crushed*
- 6 to 8 medium mushrooms, *finely sliced*
- 2 eggs
- 350ml pot crème fraîche
- 3 good handfuls grated cheddar & if you wish, some parmesan
- salt, black pepper & mustard, *to season*

You will need two 22cm loose-based tins. Preheat the oven to 180°C/350°F.

Make the shortcrust pastry by rubbing the butter into the flour until it resembles breadcrumbs. Add enough water to bring the mixture together into a dough that is soft but not sticky. Chill it in the fridge to rest.

Wash and drain the spinach – a salad spinner is excellent for this. Finely chop the onion and sweat it in some olive oil over a low heat, until it is transparent. Add the crushed garlic and mushrooms, stirring lightly. Cook these together over a very low heat until they become a soft, dark mixture; season with salt and pepper. Remove from the heat and set aside to cool.

Steam the spinach until thoroughly wilted. Drain thoroughly, pressing it hard through a sieve and removing as much liquid as you can. Chop the spinach finely and season well with salt, pepper and nutmeg.

Roll out the pastry and line the tins. Bake the pastry cases blind for 15 minutes on the middle shelf of the oven. Lightly beat the eggs. Remove the pastry cases from the oven and brush the inside with the beaten egg. Bake for a further 5 minutes or until golden.

Add the crème fraîche to the remaining beaten eggs and mix thoroughly. Fold in the mushroom, onion and garlic mixture along with the spinach and ⅔ of the cheese. Adjust the seasoning. Fill your quiche cases with the mixture and top with last third of grated cheddar and the parmesan (if using). Bake for a further 30 to 40 minutes, until your quiche is golden brown and puffy.

MALTBY STEAK & ONION PIE
serves 4

Mince and onions; it's a northern thing!

- 500g minced steak
- 1 large, or 2 small red onions
- 2 cloves garlic
- 2 sticks celery
- ¾ teaspoon sea salt, freshly ground black pepper
- ¼ teaspoon cayenne pepper
- ½ teaspoon sweet paprika

- ½ teaspoon smoked paprika
- ½ teaspoon turmeric
- 1 tablespoon Worcester Sauce
- 300ml stock (made with Marigold Bouillon powder)
- 1 tin chopped tomatoes
- 1 bay leaf

You will need a casserole dish with a lid. Preheat the oven to 150°C/300°F.

Finely chop the onion and garlic. Fry them in 2 tablespoons oil in a heavy based pan (with a lid). Add the mince and mix well while frying until everything is browned. Add the finely chopped celery, season with salt, pepper and the spices. Add the Worcester Sauce and continue to cook for a couple of minutes, stirring gently and making sure it doesn't stick and burn. Add the stock, tinned tomatoes and pop in a bay leaf or two before bringing everything to the boil.

Reduce the heat and leave to simmer on a very low heat or in a cool oven for at least an hour. This dish may be slow cooked for several hours at a very low heat.

Fill a pie dish and follow the instructions for *Aberford Pie Crust* (page 30) to top with flaky pastry and bake.

PARTICULARLY DELICIOUS APPLE CHUTNEY

makes 6 to 7 jars

This is a great addition to a sandwich filled with cheese and/or ham bought from a Yorkshire farm shop.

- 1kg cooking apples, *weighed after peeling and coring*
- 500g sultanas
- 850ml malt vinegar
- 1kg demerara sugar
- 1 teaspoon cayenne pepper
- 2 teaspoons salt
- 110g ginger, *finely chopped (weighed after peeling)*

Place the apples, sultanas and vinegar in a heavy-based saucepan and bring to the boil; simmer until soft. Leave in a cool place overnight for the sultanas to plump up.

The next day, add the remaining ingredients, bring to a rolling boil and continue boiling until the chutney begins to thicken, usually around 20 to 30 minutes. Be careful not to let it burn. Allow to cool before potting and label when completely cold.

RIEVAULX ROOT VEGETABLE CHEESY GRATIN PIE

serves 4

Vegetable pies can be fabulous too. This recipe is for a juicy, rich and sumptuous pie with a bit of crunch.

- 2 large onions, *finely chopped*
- olive oil
- 2 cloves garlic, *peeled, crushed and finely chopped*
- 1 piece of ginger, *peeled and minced*
- the leaves from 3 or 4 stalks of thyme
- ½ a swede, *cut into small flakes*
- ½ a celeriac, *cut into small flakes*
- 1 large carrot, *cut into matchsticks*
- 2 leeks, *thoroughly washed and shredded*
- 200g chopped mushrooms
- freshly ground sea salt and black pepper
- 2 or 3 handfuls of parsley, finely chopped
- 1 large mug vegetable stock, made with Marigold Bouillon powder
- 2 tablespoons crème fraîche
- 60g grated Wensleydale cheese
- 60g soft goats' cheese
- 60g walnuts, *roughly chopped (optional)*

Fry the onions over a low heat in 2 tablespoons olive oil until they are transparent. Add the garlic and ginger and cook until fragrant. Add the thyme, swede, celeriac and carrots, and gently mix before sweating the vegetables for 10 to 15 minutes. Stir the pan from time to time so they don't burn.

Add the leeks and mushrooms and stir and cook over a very low heat until they have wilted and you have a juicy mixture of softened vegetables.

Season with freshly ground sea salt and black pepper, add the parsley and pour over the stock. Bring to a gentle simmer and cook for around 15 to 20 minutes. Remove the pan from the heat and stir in the 2 tablespoons crème fraîche. Pour into a pie dish and top with the cheeses and walnuts (if using).

When cool, follow the instructions for *Aberford Pie Crust* (page 30) to top with flaky pastry and bake. Serve with an array of greens, the pie's juices make a good sauce.

ROBIN HOOD'S BAY
FISH SOUP

serves 4

This is a beautifully green soup, ideal for celebrating a day at the seaside with freshly caught fish.

- 250g smoked haddock, *(undyed)*
- 375g assorted white fish, *cut into cubes*
- 60g butter
- 1 large onion, *finely chopped*
- 1 heaped tablespoon plain flour
- 600ml milk
- 1 generous handful frozen peas
- 150ml single cream
- juice of a lemon
- salt & black pepper
- 1 handful parsley, *finely chopped*

Place the haddock in a shallow dish and pour boiling water over it. Leave it to soak for 10 minutes. In a large, heavy based pan, melt the butter and cook the onion until soft and transparent; stir in the flour and cook it for a few minutes to make a roux. Pour in 150ml of the haddock water and the milk.

Flake the haddock, reserving 2 tablespoons of haddock flakes in a

separate bowl. Add the remaining haddock, including the skin into the pan, together with the white fish cubes.

Simmer for 5 minutes, add the peas and cook for a further 5 minutes. Remove the skin and liquidize the soup.

Reheat to just below boiling point, add the cream and if necessary, thin with more of the haddock water. Season to taste with lemon, salt (sparingly) and pepper (generously). Stir in the reserved haddock flakes, parsley and serve.

ROMAN SPELT BREAD
makes 3 loaves

Yorkshire was alive with the Romans. They ate spelt loaves and they're something very special. If you're hosting Yorkshire tea parties, spelt makes really rather distinguished egg and cress, cucumber or smoked salmon sandwiches. You'd be a fool to cut off the crusts, because they are scrumptious. Spelt has a marvellous crumpety texture and a very particular malty flavour.

- I handful sea salt
- I.5kg wholemeal stoneground spelt flour
- 3 teaspoons Dove's quick yeast
- I.2 litres cold water
- 2 tablespoons sunflower oil
- I tablespoon sesame or poppy seeds

You will need three 900g bread tins. Preheat the oven to 200°C/400°F.

Put the salt, flour and yeast into a large bowl – in that order! Mix the yeast into the top of the flour keeping it well away from the salt. Make a well in the centre and add a good glug, perhaps as much as one third, of the water. Hold your jug in one hand and mix with the other. Your mixing hand will be very messy!

When the flour has absorbed that water, add the next third. Spelt makes quite a different dough from other wheat flours. It's really soft and sticky and you could panic that you've made pancake batter; it will firm up. The texture reminds me a bit of mercury, it's a semi liquid-solid state. As you work the dough round the bowl it gradually leaves the sides clean. This takes 5 to 10 minutes.

Cover the dough with a clean tea towel and leave it to rise for I to 2 hours.

Transfer a third of the dough to each tin. Each tin should be filled ⅔ full. Cover with a damp tea towel and leave to rise again until just below the top. Brush with egg and sprinkle with sesame or poppy seeds.

Bake for 45 to 50 minutes, until golden brown and sounding hollow when tapped on the bottom. These loaves are quite flat topped.

SAXON GARLIC MUSHROOMS
serves 4

The Saxons, like the Romans and Vikings, invaded and enjoyed living in Yorkshire. Apparently, they ate a lot of garlic mushrooms and this is thought to be an authentic recipe.

- 500g large flat mushrooms
- 3 to 4 large garlic cloves, *finely chopped*
- 150g butter
- 2 large handfuls parsley, *chopped*
- sea salt & freshly ground black pepper

Wipe the mushrooms clear of dirt and grit, trim the stalks. Crush the garlic to a paste with some sea salt before mixing it with the butter and parsley.

Heat about 25g butter in a heavy frying pan and place the mushrooms in them, gill side down. Cook for about 30 seconds. Turn the mushrooms over and

spoon some garlic/parsley butter into each mushroom. Grind black pepper over. Cook until the butter has melted

through the mushrooms. Watch them very carefully; it takes between 1 to 5 minutes, dependent on the size of the mushroom.

Serve with freshly baked bread to mop up the juices.

SILKSTONE STEAK
& WINTER VEGETABLE PIE
serves 4

- 500g braising steak
- 100g plain flour liberally seasoned with sea salt, black pepper, paprika, smoked paprika & turmeric
- olive oil
- 1 large onion, *finely chopped*
- 2 sticks celery, *cut into sticks or diced*
- 2 very large carrots, *cut into sticks or diced*
- ¼ medium celeriac, *cut into sticks or diced*
- ¼ medium swede, *cut into sticks or diced*

- 1 clove garlic, *finely chopped*
- a piece of root ginger about 1 inch (2.5cm) long, *finely chopped*
- 400g tin chunky chopped tomatoes in rich tomato juice
- 1 glass red wine
- 300ml stock
- 1 teaspoon mustard
- 1 bunch herbs - 1 bay leaf, the leaves from a few sprigs of thyme, lots of freshly chopped parsley and coriander
- 1 teaspoon Marigold Bouillon powder

You will need a casserole dish with a lid. Preheat the oven to 150°C/300°F.

Trim the steak and chop it into small chunks. Toss the pieces of meat in the seasoned flour, sieve off the excess and discard it. Heat the oil in a heavy-based casserole dish and brown the meat all over.

Remove the browned meat to a plate and set aside. In the casserole dish sweat the onions in 2 tablespoons oil until transparent; add the vegetables to the garlic and ginger and continue to cook gently. If needed, cover with a lid to keep all the juices in the pan.

When softened, add the meat, tomatoes, wine, stock, mustard and your bunch of herbs. Stir well. If needed,

add more seasoning and bring the dish to a gentle boil. Transfer to a low oven 150°C/300°F and simmer for at least 90 minutes or longer in needed.

Leave it to cool before filling a pie dish and follow the instructions for *Aberford Pie Crust* (page 30) to top with flaky pastry and bake.

TODMORDEN LENTIL & VEGETABLE SOUP

serves 4 to 6

The women of Todmorden have made it their mission to use waste ground to grow food for people who could not afford to eat well when Tomorden lost its industrial livelihood and suffered food poverty. They inadvertently created a worldwide movement called Incredible Edible. I think this is the sort of soup they would advocate; nourishing and full of vegetables and herbs from the garden.

- 200g puy lentils, *(soaked for 6 hours, before cooking)*
- 100g pearl barley
- 1 litre chicken or vegetable stock
- 1 large onion, *chopped*
- 2 cloves of garlic, *chopped*
- 1 x 2.5cm piece of root ginger, *chopped*
- 2 leeks, *sliced*
- 1 stick celery, *sliced*
- 2 small carrots, *sliced*
- 130g chestnut mushrooms, *sliced*
- 1 bay leaf
- 1 teaspoon turmeric, 1 teaspoon coriander, 1 teaspoon cumin
- sea salt and freshly ground black pepper
- 2 big handfuls freshly picked parsley and mint
- 1 to 2 tablespoons Tamari (Japanese fermented soy sauce)

Cook the lentils and the barley in the stock, adding enough water to make up to three times the volume of the barley, until they are tender, approximately 25 minutes.

In a separate pan, fry the onion lightly before adding the garlic and ginger, and continuing to fry until the whole mixture is softened. Add the sliced leeks, celery, carrots, mushrooms and bay leaf, and continue cooking over a low heat. When everything is softened, add the spices and mix thoroughly.

Add the vegetables to the barley, lentils and stock and simmer together for 5 to 10 minutes.

Adjust the seasoning to taste, add the freshly chopped herbs and Tamari and serve with plenty of crusty bread.

VALE OF YORK MULTI-COLOURED VEGETABLE PIE

serves 4

The tomato sauce does the work of providing steam for the perfect pie crust.

For the tomato sauce:
- 1 large onion, *finely chopped*
- olive oil
- 4 cloves of garlic, *peeled and crushed*
- a piece of root ginger, the size of a couple of walnuts, *peeled and minced*
- 1 tin finely chopped tomatoes in rich juice
- 1 tablespoon tomato puree
- the leaves from a few sprigs of thyme, *lightly chopped*
- a handful of fresh oregano leaves, *lightly chopped*
- a teaspoon of demerara sugar

For the layered vegetables:
- 2 red peppers
- 2 yellow peppers
- 200g mushrooms
- 1 handful of parsley, *chopped*
- 15g butter
- 1 large onion
- 450g spinach, *washed*
- 3 tablespoons crème fraîche
- 25g mixed breadcrumbs and Wensleydale cheese

You will need a deep cooking dish. Preheat the oven to 180°C/350°F.

Make a tomato sauce by chopping 1 onion very finely and frying it in a little olive oil until transparent. Add 2 cloves crushed, chopped garlic and the ginger. Cook over a low heat until fragrant.

Add the chopped tomatoes, tomato puree, the thyme, oregano, demerara sugar and season with salt and pepper. Bring to the boil then simmer over the lowest of heats while you prepare the rest of the dish.

Cut the peppers in half and deseed them; place them in a large tin and roast at the top of a hot oven 180°C/350°F for 15 to 20 minutes, turning them halfway through so they brown evenly. Remove from the oven and immediately place them in a plastic box with the lid on. Leave them to one side to cool.

Wash and chop the mushrooms; melt the butter before adding the mushrooms and remaining garlic and cooking for a few minutes until they begin to soften. At this point, add half the chopped parsley and season well, before cooking for a further 5 minutes or so.

Set aside and prepare the spinach.

Fry the large onion, over a low heat, in 2 tablespoons. olive oil, until transparent.

Wash the spinach thoroughly then wilt the leaves in a saucepan, with a lid on, over a low heat. Turn occasionally to make sure it doesn't burn. Now place the spinach in a sieve and leave it to stand while the liquid drains through. You may need to do this over a sink. Put a plate on top of the spinach and press down firmly to remove as much liquid as possible.

Remove the peppers from the box de-seed and peel carefully. The steam from cooking should have loosened the skins making this easy. Don't worry too much if there are small pieces of skin left on – this will add to the texture and vibrancy of the dish. Cut into generous slices.

When the spinach has drained, mix it with the onion adding 2 tablespoons of crème fraîche, the remaining parsley and seasoning with salt and pepper.

Now layer your vegetables. We want your diners to appreciate the beauty of the jewel colours. Start with spinach and onion at the bottom, next mushrooms and sliced peppers over that and top with the tomato sauce. Follow the instructions for an *Aberford Pie Crust* (page 29) to top the pie with flaky pastry. Bake in a hot oven 180°C/350°F for 15 minutes or until beautifully golden.

Serve piping hot with mashed potatoes and extra green vegetables; kale, peas and broccoli would be good.

Vale of York

VIKING GREEN SOUP
serves 4 to 6

Many people have invaded Yorkshire and the Vikings were amongst them. I've adapted this recipe for contemporary Yorkshire life.

- 1 leek sliced, *lightly sliced*
- 450g fresh spinach
- 1 knob butter
- 1 onion, *finely chopped*
- 2 cloves of garlic, *crushed and chopped*
- 1 knuckle sized piece of root ginger, *finely chopped*
- 1 litre chicken or vegetable stock

- 2 large handfuls parsley, *finely chopped*
- sea salt, freshly ground black pepper and ground ginger
- 2 to 3 egg yolks
- 200ml single cream
- freshly grated nutmeg

Wash and drain the leek and spinach separately before placing them on one side. In a little butter, sweat the onion, garlic and ginger for a few seconds before adding the leeks and cooking until soft.

Add the stock to this mixture, bring to the boil and simmer for 5 minutes.

Add the spinach and parsley and cook together, very gently, for a few minutes. Season with salt, pepper and ground ginger.

Whisk the yolks with the cream; pour into the soup while whisking briskly. Cook through.

Grate some nutmeg over the soup and serve it with a good bread.

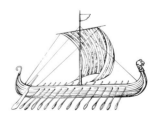

WENSLEYDALE QUICHE
serves 6

For the pastry:
- 175g plain flour
- 1 pinch of salt
- 85g butter, *cut into tiny cubes and chilled*
- a little cold water to mix

For the filling:
- 2 tablespoons light olive oil
- 1 onion, *finely chopped*
- 1 clove garlic, *crushed and chopped*
- 2 sticks celery, *finely chopped*
- 1 medium carrot, *grated*
- 1 x 300ml crème fraîche
- 2 medium free-range eggs, *lightly beaten*
- 1 handful parsley, *finely chopped*
- 110g Wensleydale cheese, *grated*

You will need a 22cm loose bottomed flan tin or fluted flan dish. Preheat the oven to 190°C/375°F.

Sieve the flour and salt into a large, cool mixing bowl. Rub in the butter until it resembles fine breadcrumbs and add the water, a little at a time, mixing gently with one hand, or the end of a round bladed knife, until you form a soft ball of dough that just stays together. Chill for about an hour before rolling.

Roll out the pastry and use to line a 22cm loose bottomed flan tin. Bake the pastry case blind at 190°C/375°F for 15 minutes on the middle shelf of the oven. Remove the pastry case from the oven and paint the inside with a little of the beaten eggs. Bake for 5 more minutes before leaving to cool.

Heat the olive oil and gently fry the onion until transparent; add the garlic, celery and carrot and cover with a lid. Sweat the vegetables together until somewhat softened. Leave to cool.

In a mixing bowl, add crème fraîche to the lightly beaten eggs and mix thoroughly. Stir in the parsley, followed by the vegetable mixture, mixing lightly but well. Sprinkle half the grated cheese over the bottom of the pastry case. Pour in your crème fraîche and vegetable mixture. Top with the other half of the grated cheese.

Bake at 190°C/375°F for 30 to 40 minutes, until your quiche is golden brown and puffy.

WHITBY SMOKED MACKEREL PÂTÉ

serves 4

Whitby is the home of Dracula and is a pilgrimage spot for his enthusiasts. This pâté is easy to prepare and makes a smashing sandwich filling or dip for raw vegetable sticks if you go out walking to admire the Abbey. Make your destination the kipper shop; nothing beats them for breakfast, with brown bread and butter.

- 3 smoked Mackerel fillets
- 1 heaped tablespoon mayonnaise
- 2 tablespoons creamy yoghurt
- 2 heaped teaspoons horseradish sauce

- juice of half a lemon
- freshly ground black pepper

Remove the skin from the smoked Mackerel. Mash/flake it into a bowl. In a separate bowl, whip up the mayonnaise, yoghurt, horseradish sauce and lemon juice. Fold in the Mackerel; stir the mixture gently to combine them evenly.

WHOLEMEAL ROLLS

makes 30 rolls

Rolls are perfect for packed lunches, on holiday outings or work days. They freeze and defrost well. Any Yorkshire farm shop will inspire you with ideas of salads, cheese, fish and ham to fill them.

- I handful sea salt
- 350g strong white stoneground organic flour
- 1.25kg strong wholemeal flour

- I sachet 7g dried yeast
- 850ml cold water
- pumpkin seeds, sunflower seeds, sesame seeds and poppy seeds

Grease, line and flour three baking trays. Preheat the oven to 220°C/425°F.

Put the salt, flours and yeast into a large bowl – in that order! Mix the yeast into the top of the flour keeping it well away from the salt. Make a well in the centre and add a good glug, perhaps as much as one third, of the water. Hold your jug in one hand and mix with the other. My experience is that wholemeal bread is less sticky and generally easier to knead than white. The same rule applies, wetter is better than drier, as it's easier to get the dough to form one cohesive ball.

Now turn the dough out onto a lightly floured worktop to knead. Dust the worktop sparingly; you might not need any flour at all to keep it moving. It's less sticky to knead than white and doesn't take as much time. There is something of the tummy about brown dough when adequately needed, but it's a denser, grainier substance, 5 to 10 minutes should do it. It's an immensely satisfying process; thoroughly good for the soul.

Scrape your bread bowl out and oil it sparingly with sunflower oil. Put the dough back in. Cover it with a clean tea towel and leave it to rise at room temperature, until it has more than doubled in size. This may take 2 to 3 hours. A long cold rise is best for the digestion. That's why I always use cold water.

Knock the dough back, by pressing it firmly, but gently and kneading well. Cut it into five roughly equal pieces. Work on one piece at a time. Divide each piece into six; they will each be approximately a handful of dough and weigh about 60g, I am obsessive and like to weigh mine for evenness and accuracy. Make each into a rough ball. Cup your hand over this ball and shape it by rotating it on the worktop so it's smoothed into a neat roll. Arrange them, well apart from each other, in rows of three then two on your baking sheet to make baker's dozen. Cover the tray with a tea towel and leave to rise until the edges are just touching.

Glaze with egg wash, sprinkle with seeds, starting with pumpkin and working in order of diminishing size.

Brush again with egg afterwards so the seeds are glued from underneath and varnished from the top. It's a messy, fiddly satisfying process, akin to a child's art and craft project.

Bake for 20 to 30 minutes, turning halfway through for even browning. You'll know they're cooked if they sound hollow when tapped underneath. Cool on a wire rack.

YORKSHIRE PUDDING

makes 12 small or 4 large plate sized puddings

Yorkshire Puddings always look fantastic and are hugely popular with adults and children alike. Outside Yorkshire they're usually served with roast beef, but here, traditionally they're a starter, served before the roast to fill up hungry tummies to curb the appetites for the more expensive meat.

Nowadays they're used as accompaniments to sweet and savoury dishes, even if this is shocking to traditionalists. All the pie fillings in this book, could alternatively be placed in big Yorkshire puds and this is frequently seen in Yorkshire pubs today.

- 175g plain flour
- salt & black pepper
- 3 free-range eggs
- 175ml milk

- 110ml water
- 2 tablespoons beef dripping or vegetable or sunflower oil (not olive oil, it can't take the heat)

You will need a 12-hole bun tin (or four 20cm cake tins). Preheat the oven to 225°C/435°F.

Place the bun tin (or cake tins), in the oven to heat, while you whip up

the batter. Sieve the flour into a large mixing bowl, or big measuring jug and grind in some sea salt and pepper. Add the eggs, the measured milk and the water (I believe strongly in the water as I think the steam is crucial to creating a good rise); whisk vigorously with an electric whisk, until you have a smooth, lump free batter.

Take the tin out of the oven and stand it on the hob, over a medium heat. Spoon the dripping or oil into the tins, to heat it. When the fat is giving off a warm haze, pour in the batter, dividing it evenly between each section.

Bake in the oven for about 20 minutes.

These little Yorkshire puddings puff up like pub Sunday lunch ones and are yummy with roast dinner and gravy.

SWEET RECIPES

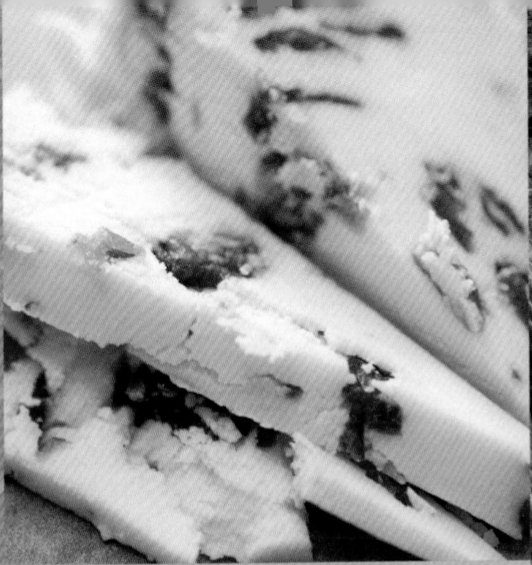

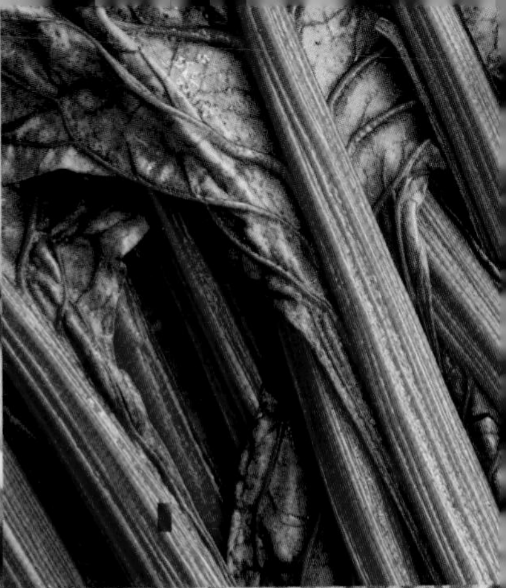

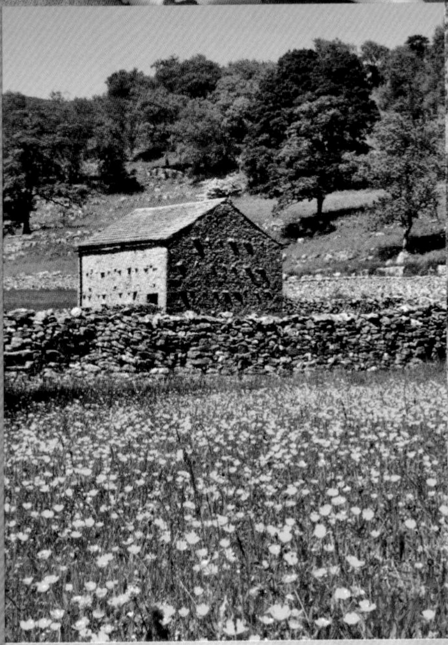

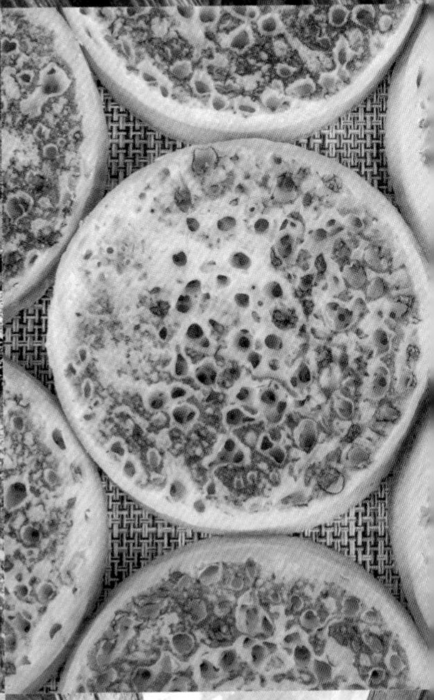

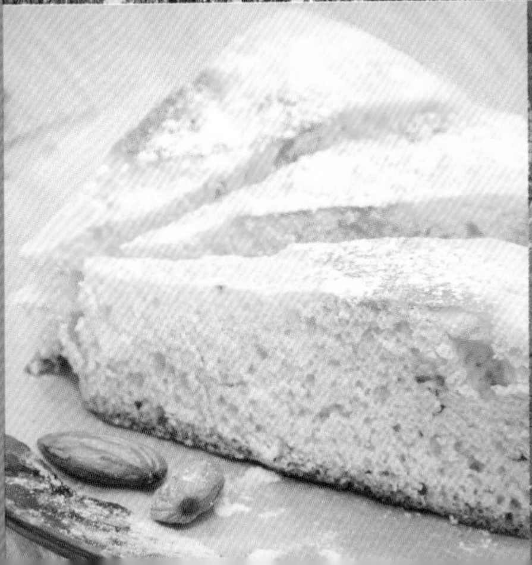

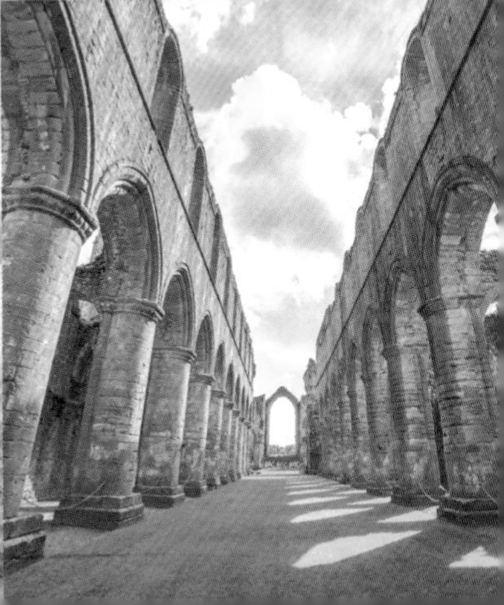

ABERFORD PIE CRUST

covers a 22cm pie dish or plate

Pies can come either with both tops and bottoms, usually made of shortcrust pastry, or with only a lid over a pie dish full of juicy, saucy insides. My experience of Yorkshire pies is the latter. The crust needs to be puffed up, golden and crispy; it must be flaky in the mouth. My mother would have made puff pastry to go on such a pie, but in my opinion, life is too short to make puff. Happily, I have an alternative flaky pastry that was taught to me by my aunt.

- 175g butter
- 225g plain flour
- a pinch of salt
- cold water - the colder the better, a few tablespoons full

Weigh out your butter, wrap it up in greaseproof paper or foil and put it in the freezer for half an hour. At the end of that time, sieve the flour and salt into a large, cold mixing bowl. Grate the butter into the flour, holding it by the foil or paper, to protect it from the warmth of your hands.

Using a palette knife, combine the butter and flour until you've made a crumbly mixture and all the butter is floury. Little by little add water and mix it in with a palette knife, until you have a soft dough that leaves the bowl clean. With your hands, gently and speedily form a single ball.

Chill it in the fridge for half an hour.

Putting a crust on a pie

Roll out the cold pastry to form a shape quite a bit bigger, at least 6cm all round than your pie dish, about the thickness of a £1 coin. Sparingly brush the pie dish's rim with water. From the excess pastry, cut a long ribbon, the width of the dish's rim, to put all along the rim. Fill the pie dish with cold filling, up to a little below the brim. Brush the pastry rim with water. Place your pastry ribbon firmly on top of the wetted rim. Lightly brush the pastry ribbon's top with water. Drape the big piece of pastry loosely and evenly over the pie. It's important not to stretch your pastry; this draping process is key to success!

Lift the pie dish, with the pastry flopping over it, on your non dominant hand, or put it on a little stand, (like a baked bean tin). Cut the pastry to shape by trimming round the edge of the dish, holding the knife at right angles to the dish and slicing.

Crimp the edges by first making little rapid horizontal cuts all around the perimeter of the pie's rim, through both layers of pastry (rim and lid); this will help them to stick together. Next, gently press your finger, just hard enough to make a tiny indentation through both layers of pastry. Using the back of a small knife in the other hand, push in the edge of the pastry, around your finger, to make a scalloped edge. Move your finger around the pie at 1.5cm intervals and repeat the scalloping, until your whole pie has a beautiful frilly edge.

Stab a small hole (about 1cm in diameter) in the centre of your pie to let out steam during cooking. Make a second ribbon of off-cut pastry into a rose (or more than one) by rolling up the strip. Stick your rose in the hole. Cut out some rose leaf shaped pieces of pastry.

Brush the pastry around the rose with water and stick on the leaves. Brush the whole lid generously with a wash of beaten egg and water. The pie is now ready to go into a hot oven or to be frozen for another day.

To heat up and bake the pie, preheat the oven to 200°C/400°F, put the glazed pie on a fairly high shelf (although not so high it will burn) and bake for about 30 minutes, turning halfway through to ensure the browning is even and the contents wonderfully cooked.

ALDFIELD ALMOND TART
serves 4 to 6

- 1 packet ready-made puff pastry
- 2 eggs – separated into yolks & whites
- 60g golden caster sugar & 1 tablespoon for sprinkling
- rind and juice of ½ an unwaxed lemon
- 30g melted butter
- 30g ground almonds
- a pinch of salt

Preheat the oven to 190°C/375°F. Line a 22cm pie plate with ready-made puff pastry.

Beat the egg yolks, caster sugar, lemon juice and rind in a large mixing bowl, with an electric hand whisk, until thick and creamy. Add the butter and almonds. Cook the mixture by placing the basin over a pan of simmering water for 10 minutes, stirring with a wooden spoon, until thick. Pour this mixture into the centre of the pie plate.

Bake for 30 minutes. While it's cooking, whisk the egg whites with the salt, until stiff. Spread over the almond mixture, sprinkle with approximately 1 tablespoon golden caster sugar. Return to the oven for about 5 to 10 minutes until set and browned. Serve warm with cream.

AMPLEFORTH APPLE PIE
serves 4

Apple pie, like motherhood, is universally recognised as the best possible thing. Serve it with custard, cream, ice cream or that most delectable indulgence – clotted cream. Yorkshire clotted cream is becoming more widely available, although south west producers will send it by post as well.

Ampleforth Abbey has celebrated orchards, with over 40 varieties of heritage apples on display to visitors.

For the filling:
- 500g cooking apples
- 2 to 3 tablespoons water
- 80g caster sugar (according to taste)
- 1 *Aberford Pie Crust*

Peel, core and slice the apples into thinnish slices (each quarter cut into around four). Place the apples into a pan and add just enough cold water to cover. Bring to a gentle simmer and cook until just soft but still holding their shape. Add the sugar.

Alternatively, put the apples in a microwaveable dish with the water and cover. Heat the apples on high for three to five minutes, so they soften but hold their shape. Add sugar according to your taste, when cooked.

When the apple mixture is cold, place in a 22cm pie dish and top with an *Aberford Pie Crust* (page 30). Brush the top of the pie with milk (not egg wash) and sprinkle it with more caster sugar before baking.

Note: Apple Pie is an incredibly versatile pudding; add a large handful of sultanas or a mixture of summer fruits (blackcurrants, blueberries and raspberries) or add mixed spices, (5 cloves, 1 teaspoon cinnamon, ¼ teaspoon ground ginger and ¼ teaspoon nutmeg) for something a little spicier.

ANLABY PARK
APRICOT PIE
serves 4

This method can be used for other stone fruits, such as cherries or plums or sour ones like gooseberries, blackcurrants or redcurrants.

- 750g apricots
- 60g unsalted butter
- 250g caster sugar

- 1 *Aberford Pie Crust*
- 1 egg white, *lightly beaten*

Preheat the oven to 200°C/400°F.

Prepare the apricots by washing, cutting in half and removing the stones.

Melt the butter and sugar in a wide based shallow pan, add the apricots and turn them over and over until thoroughly coated in the butter/sugar mixture. Heat them through, but don't let them get mushy or juicy. Pack them tightly into a circular pie dish, 22cm in diameter.

When cool, add an *Aberford Pie Crust*, (page 30) brush with egg white and sprinkle with extra caster sugar.

Bake in the oven at 200°C/400°F for 20 minutes before lowering the heat to 160°C/320°F and cooking for a further 15 minutes.

APPLE PIE
WITH CHEESE
serves 6 to 8

In Yorkshire there is a saying "an apple pie without the cheese is like a kiss without the squeeze". You could serve the Ampleforth Pie with a chunk of cheese or make the combined version below.

For the shortcrust pastry:
- 240g plain flour
- 120g butter
- cold water to mix

For the filling:
- 1kg of apples, weigh them whole before you peel and core them, *thinly sliced and cooked*
- 50g caster sugar
- 150g grated Wensleydale cheese

Make the pastry by sifting the flour into a bowl, rubbing in the butter and adding enough cold water to mix. Gather into a ball and set aside in a cool place to rest.

Cook the apples until they still have plenty of bite, add the sugar and leave to cool. Line a 22cm pie plate with the pastry and fill with layers of apple and cheese. Paint the pastry on the pie plate rim with water. Top the pie with the rest of the pastry. Cut to shape and knock up the edges to make the lid and base stay together. Flute the perimeter.

Decorate the top with a flower and leaves before brushing everything with milk and sprinkling caster sugar over the top.

Bake at 200°C/400°F for 30 mins, or until the pie is crispy and golden brown.

Wensleydale

BARDEN BRIDGE APPLE & ALMOND PICNIC CAKE

cuts into 18 pieces

- 225g plain wholemeal flour
- 1 teaspoon baking powder
- 1½ teaspoons cinnamon
- ¼ teaspoon ground nutmeg
- 1½ teaspoons mixed spice
- 110g butter, *cut up into small cubes*
- 110g almonds, *lightly ground in a blender*

- 50g soft brown sugar
- 1 lemon, *zested and juiced*
- 4 or 5 eating apples, *peeled, cored and chopped in small pieces, soaked in the juice of 1 lemon*
- 2 eggs, *lightly beaten*
- a little milk
- a spoonful or 2 of demerara sugar

Grease and line a 23cm x 34.5cm tray-bake tin. Preheat the oven to 190°C/375°F.

Sieve the flour, baking powder and spices into a large mixing bowl and rub the butter into it with your fingertips. Stir in the almonds sugar and lemon zest. Add the beaten egg, stirring through evenly but not over mixing. Peel, core and chop the apple before tossing it in the lemon juice. Add the apple to the mixture, followed by the milk, a little at a time, and stir gently until you achieve a slow, dropping consistency, i.e. a spoonful of the mixture needs a determined shake before it drops off the spoon.

Spoon the mixture into the tin and smooth the top. Sprinkle over the demerara sugar to give a crunchy top.

Bake for 35 to 40 minutes, turning once in the bake to ensure it is evenly browned. Cool in the tin before turning out on to a wire rack and leaving to cool completely, crunchy side up.

BRACK
makes 18 slices

- 300ml tea, made with 4 Yorkshire tea bags and boiling water stewed for 5 minutes
- 1 shot glass, or a decent glug, brandy, whisky, or other alcohol (optional)
- 350g mixed dried fruits, including peel
- zest and juice of a small lemon
- 275g plain flour, sifted and 2 extra tablespoons
- 2 teaspoons baking powder
- 2 teaspoons mixed spices
- 110g caster sugar
- 110g dark brown sugar
- 2 eggs, *lightly beaten*

Pour the tea into a large bowl and add the brandy (if using). Stir in the fruit, lemon zest and juice. Cover the bowl with a plate or clean tea towel and set aside to soak overnight at room temperature.

Grease and line a 1kg loaf tin or a 17.5cm square tray-bake tin with baking parchment. Preheat the oven to 160°C/320°F.

In a large mixing bowl, sieve together the dry ingredients: flour, baking powder, mixed spices and the sugars. Drain the liquid from the plumped fruit and set aside. Place the fruit on a large platter, sprinkle the 2 extra tablespoons of flour over it and sieve off the excess. If the fruits are wearing 'floury lifejackets',

they shouldn't sink in the cake mixture while it bakes.

Now slowly and gently, stir the fruit into the flour, baking powder, spice and sugar mixture. Add the beaten eggs and the tea (and alcohol if using). Stir carefully and you will have made a pretty wet batter. Pour this into the prepared tin. Bake in the middle of a preheated oven at 160°C/320°F for around 1 hour 30 minutes for the loaf version, 45 to 60 minutes for a tray-bake or until it's well risen and firm to the touch, and a skewer inserted into the middle comes out clean.

Allow to cool fully in the tin before carefully removing.

Serve spread with butter, generous quantities of Wensleydale cheese and steaming pots of Yorkshire tea.

It can be stored in an airtight container for a week or so, if it isn't eaten before that!

CHOCOLATE ORANGE BROWNIES

serves 8 greedy people

Yorkshire has over the years been home to chocolate making, both industrial and artisan. This cake is my tribute to the famous chocolate orange, manufactured first in York. It is a gluten free treat.

- 4 eggs,
- approx. 250g chocolate
- approx. 180g butter
- approx. 120g caster sugar

- approx. 60g ground almonds
- ½ teaspoon baking powder
- zest of 1 large navel orange

Grease and line a square cake tin, 25cm x 25cm, 7 cm deep. Preheat the oven to 180°C/350°F.

Weigh the 4 eggs and work out how much each one weighs individually; use the equivalent egg-weight of 4 eggs in chocolate and place this in a heatproof bowl. Take the equivalent weight of 3 eggs plus the butter. Put the butter in the same bowl as the chocolate and melt them together. When melted remove from the source of heat and let the mixture cool a little. Take the weight of 2 eggs plus the sugar, put this amount of sugar in the bowl of an electric mixer.

Leave it while you complete the weighing and preparation.

Take the equivalent weight of 1 egg plus the ground almonds, sieve the almonds with the baking powder. Take the zest off the orange and leave it to 1 side. Whip the 4 eggs up with the sugar until the mixture is very pale and fluffy. Gently combine the whipped egg mixture with the melted chocolate & butter.

Fold through the ground almonds and finally the orange zest.

Pour the cake batter into the prepared tin and bake in the centre of the preheated oven for 40 minutes, turning halfway through if required for even distribution of heat. When it's ready, a skewer inserted into the centre comes out clean. Leave to cool in the tin for about 10 minutes, then turn out to cool completely on a wire rack.

CHOCOLATE YORKSHIRE PUDDING PROFITEROLES

serves 12

This is surely not a dish for the purist, but it tickled my sense of humour and the taste buds of my sons and nephew.

- 225g batter
- 225g plain flour
- 4 eggs, *beaten*
- 1 teaspoon sugar
- 400ml milk
- 2 tablespoons cold water

- 12 teaspoons vegetable oil
- 300ml double cream
- 100g dark chocolate, *roughly chopped*
- 150ml double cream
- a pinch of salt

Preheat the oven to gas 240°C/475°F. Warm up a 12 hole bun tin.

Sift the flour into a wide jug, add the sugar and salt, add the eggs and liquid and whip up with an electric whisk or stick blender, until smooth. Put 1 teaspoon of oil into each section of the hot bun tin and a couple of tablespoons of batter on it. Put the bun tin on the highest shelf of the oven and bake for 20 minutes, or until the puddings are golden, crispy and well risen.

Whip up 300ml double cream.

To make the Ganache
Melt the chocolate and cream stirring constantly until you achieve a thick sauce consistency.

Cool the puddings on a wire rack. When completely cool, put a dessert spoonful of cream in each, make a mountain of cream filled puddings on a glamorous serving dish. Serve with the chocolate ganache. I found it entertaining to put my chocolate sauce in a gravy boat.

CURD TARTS
makes 8 individual or 1 large tart(s)

For the pastry:
- 175g plain flour
- 85g butter, *cut into tiny cubes and chilled*
- a little cold water to mix
- a pinch of salt

- 1.2 litre full milk and the juice of 1 lemon or 225g curd cheese
- 50g unsalted butter
- 2 eggs, *separated*
- 50g caster sugar
- grated rind of 1 lemon and a good squeeze of its juice
- 25g currants (optional, I opt out)
- 1 teaspoon grated nutmeg

For the filling:

Preheat the oven to 180°C/350°F.

Grease & flour 8 little bun tins, 7cm diameter, 3cm deep, (I also put paper muffin liners in mine as I worry they'll stick) or 1 large 20cm tin.

If you feel the need to make the curds, do it the night before, by heating the milk in a large saucepan over a low heat and bringing it to a very gentle simmer. Remove from the heat. Pour in the lemon juice and stir a couple of times, to help the curds form. Set aside to cool for an hour. Line a sieve with muslin (or a clean tea towel) and place over a large bowl. Pour the contents of the pan, now curds and whey, into the sieve and leave it to drain in the fridge overnight.

Make the shortcrust pastry by sieving the flour and salt into a large, cool mixing bowl, rubbing in the butter until it resembles fine breadcrumbs and adding water, a little at a time, and mixing gently with one hand, or the end of a round bladed knife, until you form a soft ball of dough that just stays together. Chill the pastry for about an hour before rolling it out and cutting it into 8 circles with a 9.8cm cutter. Carefully fit the circles of pastry into the tins, prick the bases with a fork and leave the prepared uncooked tart cases in the fridge.

Melt the butter, beat it together with egg yolks, sugar, the lemon zest, juice and the curd cheese; mix in the currants (if using) and half the nutmeg. In a separate bowl whisk the egg whites until stiff and fold into the egg yolk mixture.

Fill the 8 pastry cases and sprinkle the tops with the rest of the nutmeg. Bake at 180°C/350°F for 15 to 20 minutes until the filling is just set.

FAT RASCALS

makes 8 Rascals

For the rascals:
- 175g plain flour
- 175g self raising flour
- 1 teaspoon ground cinnamon
- ½ teaspoon ground nutmeg
- 1 teaspoon baking powder
- 150g cold butter, *cubed*
- 85g golden caster sugar
- 225g mixed dried fruit: currants, sultanas, raisins and cut mixed peel
- 2 eggs, *lightly beaten*
- grated zest of 1 orange and 1 lemon
- juice of half a large or 1 small lemon
- juice of half a large or 1 small orange
- 80 to 100ml milk

For the glaze:
- 1 medium egg yolk
- 1 tablespoon water

For the decorating:
- Glacé cherries
- whole blanched almonds

Grease and line a large baking sheet. Preheat the oven to 200°C/400°F.

Sieve the flours, spices and baking powder into a large mixing bowl. Rub in the butter until it resembles fine breadcrumbs. Add the sugar, mixed dried fruit, eggs, zests and fruit juice. Mix gently adding enough milk to make a soft ball of dough. When lightly combined, divide the mixture into eight equal balls, each about the size of a medium orange, and place on a greased and lined large baking sheet. Flatten into buns about 2cm, ¾ inch deep.

Mix the egg yolk and water together and use as a glaze for the tops of the buns. Decorate with the almonds and cherries to look like little rascally faces! Bake at 200°C/400°F for 15 to 20 minutes until golden. Cool on a wire rack and serve with a pot of Yorkshire tea.

HORSFORTH FLAPJACKS

makes 36 flapjacks

This is really my mother, Barbara's, flawless flapjack recipe. My sister has been making them in Horsforth since 1979, so they're Yorkshire natives now and are ideal as a packed lunch pudding. This recipe uses two types of oats which I think makes the texture perfect, but it's not vital.

- 360g butter
- 270g demerara sugar
- 90g golden syrup
- 240g porridge oats

- 240g jumbo oats
- 120g sunflower seeds
- 120g pumpkin seeds
- 120g sesame seeds

Grease and line two swiss roll tins, with baking parchment. Preheat the oven to 150°C/300°F.

Place the butter, sugar and golden syrup into a bowl and whisk until they become light and golden. Add the oats and seeds and stir carefully to avoid breaking them up. Divide the mixture between the two greased and lined swiss roll tins and spread carefully, remembering to fill even the remotest corners of each tin. 'Rough up' the surface a little with a fork. Bake in the centre of the oven at 150°C/300°F for 25 to 30 minutes, turning halfway through baking for even browning.

Remove the tins from the oven and mark out 18 fingers in each tin. Make two rows, by cutting along the middle, horizontally and nine columns, by cutting into three lengthwise and then each third into three again. This will make them as equal as you can without a ruler. Turn the oven off and return the tins to the cooling ovens to allow the flapjacks to crisp up. When completely cold, turn out onto a cooling rack and snap into fingers.

Pop one into your packed lunch with the haverbread wraps and an apple from Ampleforth!

PARKIN
makes 16 slices

- 110g dark brown soft sugar
- 160g golden syrup
- 160g black treacle
- 115g butter
- 2 teaspoons finely chopped fresh root ginger
- 150g plain wholemeal flour
- 150g plain flour

- 175g medium oatmeal - pinhead oatmeal or steel cut
- ¼ teaspoon salt
- 2 teaspoons ground ginger
- 1 teaspoon cinnamon
- ½ teaspoon ground nutmeg
- 1 teaspoon bicarbonate of soda
- 125ml milk
- 2 medium eggs, *lightly beaten*

Grease and line a 17.5cm square tin. Preheat the oven 150°C/300°F.

Weigh the sugar, syrup and treacle directly into the pan before adding the butter and heating gently until the mixture melts and becomes a rich smelling syrupy mixture. Add the chopped root ginger and stir well. Cool the mixture slightly. Sieve the flours, oatmeal, salt, ginger, cinnamon and nutmeg into a large bowl, mix together and make a well in the centre.

In a bowl, dissolve the bicarbonate of soda in a couple of teaspoons of the milk before adding the egg and the rest of the milk and mixing enthusiastically. Combine this with the melted mixture. Beat well with a spoon to form a batter. Pour the batter into the well in the flour/oat/spices bowl and fold it all together.

Pour the batter into the prepared tin. Bake in the centre of the oven for about 1 hour until firm to the touch or the mixture starts to shrink from the sides of the tin. Remove from the oven and cool in the tin for 10 minutes before transferring to a cooling rack.

When cold, store in a cake tin. Parkin is best left for a few days before eating as this allows it to become slightly sticky and the flavours to develop. However, it may not get this opportunity!

PIKELETS
makes 10 to 12 Pikelets

Linda Collister, celebrated aficionado of bread and yeast cookery says, "as fond as I am of crumpets, I prefer pikelets, their northern cousins." Try these out after a bracing walk in the hills. They'll warm you through.

- 310g white or wholemeal self raising flour
- 85g caster sugar
- 1 large egg

- 340ml milk
- 85g unsalted butter
- 1 teaspoon white wine vinegar
- ¼ teaspoon bicarbonate of soda

Sift the flour and sugar into a bowl. Add the egg and milk to make a thick batter (like a cake mixture, so add a little extra milk if necessary), whisking well to avoid lumps.

Melt the butter, then add the vinegar and bicarbonate of soda and quickly mix the whole lot into the batter. Drop a few spoonfuls of batter onto a hot, lightly greased frying pan.

Cook until bubbles appear on the surface and the bottoms are browned. Flip over and cook the other side. Repeat with the remaining batter.

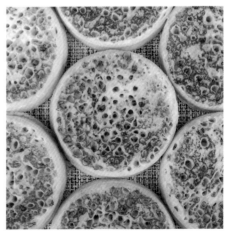

Eat immediately or, if you choose, store the pikelets in the refrigerator and toast lightly when you wish to eat them.

Delicious spread with fresh, local butter.

RASPBERRY MACAROONS

makes 13 macaroons (two halves sandwiched together) or 26 single macaroons

There is a great debate over whether these are macarons or macaroons, with some saying that the addition of colour changes a macaron into a macaroon and others arguing that only the addition of coconut can make a macaroon. Whatever you call them, these are advertised as the reason to go out for tea in a celebrated Yorkshire tea shop. I opted for no artificial colours and flavours.

For the Macaroons:
- 3 large egg whites at room temperature
- 225g golden icing sugar
- 175g ground almonds
- 5 teaspoons freeze dried raspberries (these are easily available in supermarkets)
- 2 tablespoons water
- a pinch of salt

- 2 egg yolks
- 50g granulated sugar
- 1 tablespoon flour
- 200ml milk
- 3 drops Foodie Flavours raspberry natural flavouring
- 3 drops vanilla extract

For the filling:
Preheat the oven to 160°C/320°F.

Line two baking trays with baking parchment each one with 13 well-spaced circles, 4cm diameter, drawn on each.

To make the Macaroons
Using a sparklingly clean bowl, whisk the egg whites and salt until stiff. Pulse the icing sugar, ground almonds and freeze dried raspberries to a fine powder in a food processor, before sieving them twice to remove any remaining pieces. This takes a little time, effort and determination, but is well worth it. Add this mixture into the egg whites and continue stirring until you have a smooth and glossy mixture.

For an informal look, drop 13 teaspoonfuls on to each baking tray; they will come out looking like flat, shiny pennies when baked. However, if you prefer, pour the macaroon mixture into a piping bag and pipe the mixture into the drawn circles.

Give the baking tray a sharp tap, to help the mixture settle. Set the tray aside at room temperature for 30 minutes. In this time, a light non-sticky top will form. Bake in the preheated oven for approximately 13 minutes, until glossy and firm.

Allow to cool before gently peeling the macaroons away from the baking parchment.

To make the filling

Whisk the yolks and sugar together in a large mixing bowl until thick and pale. Stir in the flour.

Heat the milk, with the raspberry flavouring and bring it to the boil. Pour this milky mixture on to the eggs and stir well. Pour the combined mixture through a sieve and back into a clean saucepan. Reheat the mixture, stirring continuously until it thickens. Cover and chill until you are ready to prepare the macaroons for serving.

To serve: sandwich two macaroons together, by holding one shell flat side up and spreading on a layer of custard. Stick the second shell on top. Serve with raspberries and whipped cream.

RHUBARB

Rhubarb is Yorkshire through and through. The Rhubarb triangle is in west Yorkshire, between Wakefield, Morley and Rothwell. It's locally known as the Tusky Triangle, tusky being the Yorkshire word for rhubarb. Like Stilton cheese, Cornish clotted cream and Melton Mowbray pork pie, Yorkshire forced rhubarb has a Protected Designation of Origin status.

Until the mid-twentieth century, there was even a 'rhubarb express train', which ran annually from Christmas until Easter, taking harvested rhubarb from Yorkshire to London for sale in Covent Garden.

Rhubarb has received somewhat of a boost in recent years, with well-known chefs championing its sweet flavour, tenderness and versatility. To my mind, there are a couple of tip top puddings everyone should make with it.

ROTHWELL RHUBARB & CUSTARD TART

serves 6

I found this recipe many years ago. In my experience, even people who think they don't like rhubarb, gleefully gobble second helpings of it.

For the pastry:
- 150g plain flour
- 100g unsalted butter, *cut into little cubes and chilled*
- 1 tablespoon caster sugar
- 1 small egg separated
- 2 tablespoons ice cold water
- a pinch salt

For the filling:
- 600g trimmed rhubarb
- 3 tablespoons caster sugar
- 250ml crème fraîche
- 2 large egg yolks
- 1 teaspoon vanilla extract

You will need a 23cm diameter, 3.5cm high fluted tart dish. Preheat the oven to 190°C/375°F.

Begin by sieving the flour and salt into a large mixing bowl, adding the diced butter and gently rubbing it into the flour until the mixture resembles fine breadcrumbs. Stir in the sugar before adding the egg yolk and water and mixing carefully until dough comes together. Turn out onto a lightly floured surface and flatten into a disc. Chill for at least 1 hour.

While the pastry is chilling, prepare the filling by cutting the rhubarb into 1.5cm lengths and mixing it with two heaped tablespoons sugar. Tip mixture onto a baking tray and bake in centre of oven at 190°C/375°F for 15 to 20 minutes or until just beginning to soften. Set aside to cool.

Place a solid baking sheet in centre of oven to heat up. Roll out pastry and line a 23cm diameter, 3.5cm high fluted tart tin. Brush the pastry with a little egg white and chill for 20 minutes. Prick it all over with a fork. Bake the pastry case blind, on the hot baking sheet at 190°C/375°F for 15 minutes until golden brown. Remove from the oven and reduce the temperature to 180°C/350°F.

Now make the filling by beating together the crème fraîche, egg yolks, vanilla and the remaining tablespoon of caster sugar. Arrange the rhubarb on the base of the tart case and pour over the creamy mixture. Bake for a further 30 minutes until the custard has set and the top is golden in places.

Remove from the oven and cool to room temperature before serving.

RAWSTONSTALL RHUBARB CRUMBLE
serves 4

Crumble is the simplest, most ubiquitous pudding. For me, it is served with custard, cream, ice cream or even Cornish clotted cream and it should always be hot enough to make cream melt.

To make your crumble into a prized tasty treat, not a boring poor pudding, my top tips are:
Use self raising flour as it makes the topping more 'cakey'. This is how my mum made it although it was not what I was taught in school or often used in cookery books; use a proper pie dish, which is at least 3.2cm deep. You need twice the depth of stewed fruit to crumble and the fruit should be juicy. The crumble should be an island of 'duff' on a pool of fruit. Crumble is definitely a pudding in a bowl, not a tart on a plate.

For the stewed rhubarb:
- 500g trimmed rhubarb
- 4 to 5 tablespoons caster sugar
- a little water

For the crumble:
- 175g self raising flour
- 110g butter, *cut into cubes and kept cold until use*
- 50g caster sugar and extra for dusting

You will need a deep pie dish. Preheat the oven to 180°C/350°F.

Wash the rhubarb and cut it into 2cm lengths before placing it in a solid based pan, adding 4 tablespoons of caster sugar, a little water and simmering gently, covered with a lid, until tender. Be careful not to over-cook the rhubarb - you want bright pink fruit. Set aside to cool.

Sieve the flour into a large mixing bowl. Drop the butter into the flour and gently rub it in with your fingertips until the mixture resembles fine breadcrumbs. Stir in the sugar.

Place the fruit in bottom of a lightly buttered pie dish and cover with the crumble mixture. Sprinkle with a dusting of caster sugar.

Bake at 180°C/350°F for 20 minutes or until golden and bubbling at the edges.

SUSAN SOWERBY'S CURRANT BUNS

makes 26 buns

In Frances Hodgson Burnett's The Secret Garden, Susan sends clandestine supplies of food to Mary and Colin. They love her currant bread. The recipe isn't included in the story, so I invented this one. The citrus glaze will give you a zing of energy, like the moorland air that brought roses to the children's cheeks.

- 1 pot of Earl Grey tea
- 100g sultanas
- 600g stoneground white bread flour
- 1 scant dessertspoon salt
- 100g soft brown sugar
- 1 teaspoon cinnamon
- ½ teaspoon ground ginger
- ½ teaspoon mixed spice
- 1 lemon, zest only
- 1 orange, zest only

- 2 sachets 7g active dried baking yeast
- 75g butter
- 425ml milk
- water as required
- 2 beaten eggs

For the icing:
- 50g icing sugar
- 2 tablespoons orange juice
- zest of 1 small lemon

Grease and line one large or two standard size baking trays with baking parchment. Preheat the oven to 200°C/400°F.

Make a strong pot of tea and leave it to rest for 5 minutes before pouring. Soak the sultanas in the tea, ideally overnight. Drain them and discard the tea.

Sift the flour, salt, brown sugar, spices, lemon and orange zests in a large bowl. Stir in the yeast. Melt the butter in the milk, but don't over-heat. Beat the eggs lightly.

Mix the dry and wet ingredients with your hand until you have made a soft dough. Turn the dough out on to a lightly floured worktop and knead it until it feels silky. Leave to rise in a fresh bowl, covered with a clean tea towel, at room temperature until it doubles in size.

Turn the dough back onto a minimally floured surface, press it down gently and cut into 26 equal pieces. Roll them into neat roll shapes. Arrange the buns on the baking tray in a baker's dozen (13 pieces/tray), cover with a damp, clean tea towel and leave to rise until they have doubled in size and are touching each other. Bake in the preheated oven for approximately 25 minutes or until they are golden brown.

Make a thin icing glaze by sifting the icing sugar into a bowl, stir in the lemon zest and enough freshly squeezed orange juice to form a thin custard consistency. You can paint this over the buns when they're still warm or wait until they're cold if you prefer.